The Story of a Special Day
Volume 255

September

11

The 254th day of the year (255th in leap years).
There are 111 days remaining until the end of the year.

by Michael Dobson

Timespinner
Press

This book is also available in e-book form for Kindle, e-pub devices, and other formats from your favorite online booksellers.

For more information about the series, about us, or about your special day, please email us at editor@timespinnerpress.com.

Look for other volumes in *The Story of a Special Day*, coming often. See www.timespinnerpress.com for details and for the most recent information.

Table of Contents

For the definition of "OS," "CE," and "BCE" used with
some dates , see the section "On Names and Dates."

Quote of the Day

"Only tragedy allows the release of love
and grief not normally seen."

Kate Bush, singer-songwriter

Today in History

September 11

Firefighters at the World Trade Center on 9/11

Event of the Day
September 11, 2001 — Terrorist Attacks Against the US

On Tuesday morning, September 11, 2001, four airliners were hijacked by terrorists affiliated with al-Qaeda (القاعدة), an Islamic militant group, and used to attack New York City's World Trade Center, the Pentagon, and at least one other Washington, DC, target.

The attacks killed 2,996 people, injured over 6,000 more, caused at least $10 billion in property and infrastructure damage, and an estimated $3 trillion in various associated costs. It was also the deadliest incident for firefighters and law enforcement officers in US history, with over 400 killed.

Often referred to as simply "9/11," the event had long-ranging consequences for all sides.

Background

The organization that eventually became known as al-Qaeda was first organized in Afghanistan by Saudi Arabian Osama bin Laden, with the original goal of resisting the Soviet occupation of that country. Over $600 million in US aid (funneled through Pakistan) helped support that effort; at least some of those funds went in support of bin Ladin's efforts.

With the Soviet withdrawal from that country, al-Qaeda turned its eye toward Islamic struggles around the world. He issued a proclamation calling for US withdrawal from Saudi Arabia and provided financial and other support to numerous other groups. He established a headquarters and training camp in Afghanistan, with at least the tacit acceptance of the Taliban government of Afghanistan.

Bin Ladin began his attacks on the US with an unsuccessful 1996 attempt to assassinate President Bill Clinton in Manila, followed by a 1998 bombing of US embassies in East Africa, killing 224. In 2000, al-Qaeda forces in Yemen bombed the USS Cole, a missile destroyer, killing 17. They then began planning for a strike against the United States.

The Plot

The actual plan for the 9/11 attacks was originally presented by Khalid Sheikh Mohammed, a senior al-Qaeda leader. Once approved, it was given leadership and financial support from the organiation.

Pilots for the suicide mission were enrolled in flight schools in the United States, and they were joined by others in the conspiracy. The US government became aware that a major attack was in the works, but not the details.

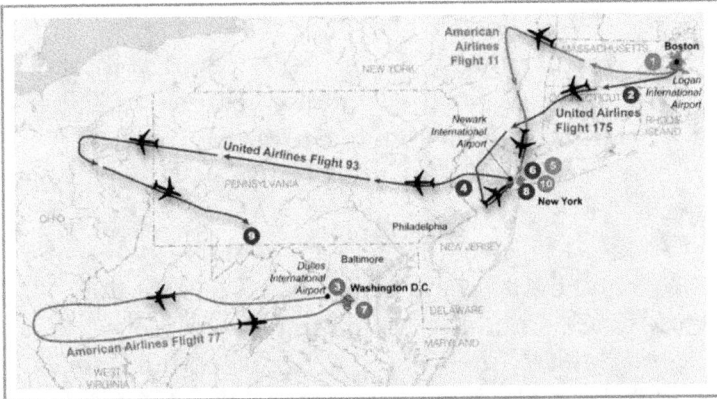

Map showing flight paths of the hijacked airplanes on 9/11.

Key:

❶ 7:59 a.m. American Airlines Flight 11, departs Boston

❷ 8:14 a.m. United Airlines Flight 175, departs Boston

❸ 8:20 a.m. American Airlines Flight 77, departs Washington

❹ 8:42 a.m. United Airlines Flight 93, a Boeing 757, departs Newark

❺ 5 8:46 a.m. American 11 crashes into the North Tower of the World Trade Center

❻ 9:03 a.m. United 175 crashes into the South Tower

❼ 9:37 a.m. American 77 crashes into the Pentagon

❽ 9:59 a.m. The South Tower collapses

❾ 10:03 a.m. United 3 crashes in Shanksville, Pennsylvania

❿ 10:28 a.m. The North Tower collapses.

The Attacks

On the morning of September 11, 2001, a total of 19 hijackers took control of four commercial airliners. Two originated in Boston, one came from Washington, and the last took off from Newark, New Jersey.

At 8:46 am, five hijackers crashed the first plane, American Flight 11, into the North Tower of the World Trade Center in Manhattan. Seventeen minutes later, United Flight 175 crashed into the South Tower. Half an hour later, American Flight 77, which originated at Washington Dulles, crashed into the Pentagon, causing heavy damage to the western side of the building.

Firefighters at the Pentagon on 9/11

The fourth flight, United Flight 93, which had taken off from New Jersey, was on its way to Washington, DC, with a target believed to be either the Capitol or the White House when passengers and crew, who knew their likely fate, fought back and tried to seize control of the plane. Before they could do so, however, the hijackers rolled the plane over and crashed it, killing all aboard.

Meanwhile, the twin towers of the World Trade Center continued to burn. About an hour after it was hit, the South Tower collapsed due to fire-induced structural failure. Half an hour later, the North Tower also collapsed. Debris from the North Tower damaged the neighboring 7 World Trade Center building, and it too collapsed about seven hours later.

Aftermath

The attack claimed a total of 2,996 lives. In addition to the 265 people on the four planes, 125 died at the Pentagon, and 2,606 in the World Trade Center and surrounding areas. There 345 firefighters, 72 law enforcement officers, and 55 military personnel among the dead. Over 90 countries lost citizens in the attack. Over 6,000 people were injured, many seriously. The site itself remained toxic for a long time.

Immediate rescue operations began, even though the site was still hazardous. Round-the-clock operations lasted for months.

The outcry was worldwide, but especially so in the United States. A number of emergency measures were put in place immediately, followed by federal action to assist victims and to increase security within the US, primarily in the form of the USA PATRIOT Act. An upsurge in hate crimes against Muslims and anyone perceived to be of Middle Eastern origins also took place.

The United States responded with diplomatic and military force, known overall as the War on Terror. They first toppling the Taliban government in Afghanistan for their harboring of al-Qaeda. A special detention camp in Guantanamo Bay, Cuba, was set up to imprison those classified as "illegal enemy combatants."

The subsequent US invasion of Iraq was also justified as a response to Islamic militant attacks and especially to al-Qaeda. Bin Ladin himself eluded capture for a number of years, and was finally killed by US Navy SEALs in Abbotabad, Pakistan, in 2011.

Memorial

On the site of the Twin Towers, a new building, One World Trade Center, finished construction in 2014, claiming the title of tallest building in the Western Hemisphere. Both the Trade Center complex and the Pentagon feature memorials to the attacks. Another memorial is (at the time of writing) planned for the crash site of United 93.

The anniversary of the attacks is now known as Patriot Day, with memorial services at all three sites.

The new One World Trade Center under construction in 2011.
(Photo: Kai Brinker)

The Blue Diamond of the Crown of France (known as the "French Blue") in its "toison" setting. (Illustration by François Farges)

What Happened on September 11?

From great works of engineering and art to devastating wars and natural disasters, thousands of years of history have left their mark on each and every day of the year. Here are some important events that occurred on September 11. (Items with a photo or illustration are boxed.)

1297 — In the **Battle of Stirling Bridge**, a Scottish force of 6,000 wins a decisive victory over 9,000 British troops. The film *Braveheart* shows a version of this battle, but it's missing the actual bridge.

1609 — Dutch explorer **Henry Hudson**, namesake of the Hudson River, **discovers Manhattan** Island.

1776 — In an attempt to end the Revolutionary War, British officials meet with representatives of the Continental Congress, including John Adams and Benjamin Franklin. The **Staten Island Peace Conference** broke apart after three hours, and the war continued.

1792 — The **French crown jewels are stolen** during a five day looting spree during the Reign of Terror. While eventually many of the jewels were recovered, the 69-carat stone known as the French Blue was not. That stone was cut into two pieces, one of which is the famous 45-carat **Hope Diamond,** on display at the Smithsonian Institution.

1857 — The Nauvoo Legion, a militia made up of southern Utah Mormon settlers, slaughters over 100 wagon train emigres in the culmination of the **Mountain Meadows massacre**, which began September 7.

1972 — San Francisco's Bay Area Rapid Transit System (**BART**) begins passenger service.

1973 — A coup in **Chile** led by General Augusto **Pinochet** overthrows the government of Salvador **Allende**. Pinochet rules as dictator until finally ousted in 1990.

1985 — Baseball player **Pete Rose** hits for the 4,192th time, **breaking Ty Cobb's record** for most career hits.

2007 — The Russian Air Force tests the Aviation Thermobaric Bomb of Increased Power, nicknamed the **Father of All Bombs.** It is reported to be the most powerful non-nuclear weapon in the world, four times as destructive as the previous record-holder, which carried the nickname "Mother of All Bombs."

2012 — Members of the militant group Ansar al-Sharia attack the US diplomatic compound in **Benghazi,** resulting in two deaths, including the American Ambassador, J. Christopher Stevens, as well as several official investigations.

Augusto Pinochet

Salvador Allende

Quote of the Day

"A story with a moral appended is like the bill of a mosquito. It bores you, and then injects a stinging drop to irritate your conscience."

O. Henry, short-story writer
born September 11, 1862

Births and Deaths

September 11

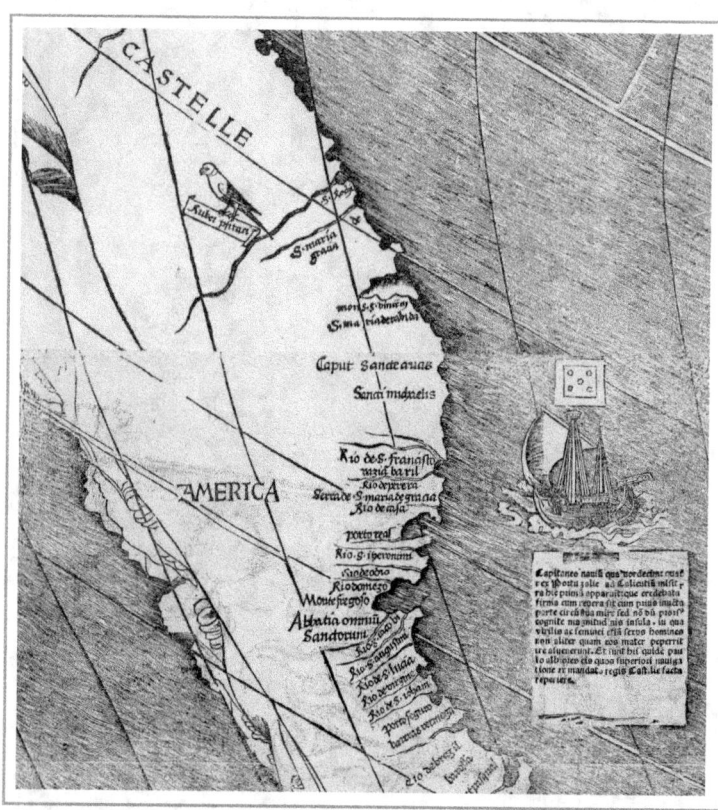

A 1507 map by Martin Waldseemüller, featuring the word "America" used in print for the first time. Waldseemüller was born on September 11, 1470.

Notable September 11 People

With the current world population at about seven billion people, on average about 19 million people also celebrate their birthdays on September 11 — and that isn't counting millions and millions who came before! No matter when you were born, you share your birthday with many special people whose accomplishments (and occasionally embarrassments) have been noted as part of history.

In this section, you'll meet fascinating people who share your birthday. They're organized by what they're famous for, and then in reverse chronological order from most recent to earliest. Those who are shown in photographs or artwork have a box around them. We don't have photos of everyone, so please forgive us if your favorite person is missing.

Some of these people you've heard of, others will be new to you, but they all make up an important part of the reason that September 11 is a truly special day!

Moldov mp honoring cosmonaut Gherman Titov

Who Was Born on September 11?

Art and Illustration

Jean-Claude Forest, French comic book writer and illustrator best known for his character *Barbarella.* *(1930)*

Crime and Punishment

Felix Dzerzhinsky (Фе́ликс Дзержи́нский), Bolshevik revolutionary who established the Soviet secret police and directed their operations for many years. *(1877*)*

Hawley Harvey Crippen, known as "Dr. Crippen," hanged for the murder of his wife in a highly sensationalized case, which has been portrayed in film, television, and novels. *(1862)*

Exploration and Discovery

Gherman Titov (Герман Титов), Soviet cosmonaut, second human to orbit the Earth and fourth human in space. *(1935)*

---

* "Old Style" dates use the Julian calendar, while "New Style" dates use the modern Gregorian calendar. Russia adopted the new calendar in 1918, resulting in two dates for some events. See "What Day of the Week is September 11?" for more detail.

Martin Waldseemüller, German mapmaker credited with the first recorded use of the word "America," on a map he created in 1507. He chose the name in honor of the explorer Amerigo Vespucci, who was the first to show that the landmass discovered by Columbus was not part of Asia, but consisted of continents in their own right. *(1470) (Photo page 14.)*

Journalism and Literature

Jessica Mitford, author and activist, known for her coverage of the American civil rights movement and for her book *The American Way of Death*. She was one of the Mitford sisters, highly public figures in England. *(1917)*

Alvar Lidell, famous BBC radio announcer and newsreader during the Second World War. His opening, "Here is the news, and this is Alvar Lidell reading it," became a national catchphrase. *(1908)*

D. H. Lawrence, novelist, poet, and critic, known for *Lady Chatterly's Lover,* considered at the time to be highly scandalous. *(1885)*

O. Henry, American short story writer known for his surprise endings; famous works include "The Gift of the Magi" and "The Ransom of Red Chief." *(1862)*

Fitz Hugh Ludlow, explorer and journalist in the American West, known for his autobiographical work *The Hasheesh Eater. (1836)*

O. Henry (real name William Sydney Porter), circa 1916

Harry Connick, Jr.

Military

Donald Blakeslee, American fighter pilot who flew with the Royal Canadian Air Force and the Royal Air Force Eagle Squadron prior to US entry into World War II, then became a squadron leader in the US Army Air Force. He flew more combat missions against the Luftwaffe than any other American. *(1917)*

Music

Ludacris, hip hop recording artist and actor who has won Screen Actors Guild Awards, Grammys, and MTV Awards. *(1977)*

Jonny Buckland, lead guitarist and co-founder of Coldplay. *(1977)*

Harry Connick Jr., jazz big band leader and singer ranked among the best-selling recording artists in the US. *(1967)*

Moby, singer-songwriter, producer, and musician known for electronica, house music, and alt rock. *(1965)*

Tony Gilroy, screenwriter and filmmaker who wrote the first four *Bourne* films (and directed the fourth), co-wrote *Rogue One: A Star Wars Story;* nominated for Academy Awards for *Michael Clayton* and *Duplicity.* *(1956)*

Tommy Shaw, singer-songwriter and guitarist best known as a member of Styx. *(1953)*

Mickey Hart, best known as one of the two drummers of the Grateful Dead. *(1943)*

Jack Ely, musician best known as the lead singer on the Kingsmen's 1963 hit "Louie, Louie." *(1943)*

Lola Falana, popular singer, dancer, and actress, known as the "Black Venus." *(1942)*

Jimmie Davis, popular country music and gospel singer who served as governor of Louisiana from 1944 to 1948 and again from 1960 to 1964. As a musician, his best-known hit was "You Are My Sunshine." Member of the Country Music Hall of Fame. *(1899)*

Herbert Stothart, won the Academy Award for Best Original Score for *The Wizard of Oz;* also wrote popular songs, including "I Wanna Be Loved By You."

James Thomson, poet and playwright remembered for writing the lyrics to the British patriotic song "Rule, Britannia." *(1700)*

Performing Arts

Kristy McNichol, actress known for roles in the TV series *Family* and *Empty Nest,* and for the film *Little Darlings. (1962)*

Lola Falana (with Gino Bramieri)

Kristy McNichol

Virginia Madsen, actress nominated for both an Academy Award and a Golden Globe for *Sideways;* other films include *Dune, Candyman, Gotham, The Rainmaker,* and *Ghosts of Mississippi. (1961)*

Amy Madigan, nominated for an Academy Award for the 1985 film *Twice in a Lifetime;* won a Golden Globe for the 1989 TV film *Roe vs. Wade. (1950)*

Brian De Palma, director of such films as *Carrie, Dressed to Kill, The Untouchables,* and *Mission: Impossible. (1940)*

Cathryn Damon, actress known for such sitcoms as *Soap* and *Webster. (1930)*

Earl Holliman, actor best known as Sgt. Crowley on the 1970s television series *Police Woman. (1928)*

Herbert Lom, actor best remembered for his role as Chief Inspector Dreyfus in the *Pink Panther* film series. *(1917)*

Politics

Bashar al-Assad (بشار الأسد), president of Syria following the death of his predecessor and father, whose crackdowns on demonstrators triggered the Syrian Civil War. *(1965)*

Ferdinand Marcos, president of the Philippines from 1965 to 1986; ruled under martial law from 1972 to 1981. *(1917)*

Ferdinand and Imelda Marcos (Photo: Al Ramones and Domie
Quiazon, courtesy US Army)

Science and Technology

Hiroshi Amano (天野 浩), Japanese physicist and inventor who shared the 2014 Nobel Prize in Physics for advances in LED technology. *(1960)*

Carl Zeiss, German manufacturer of high quality lenses and optical devices from microscopes to planetariums; founded the company of the same name. *(1816)*

Sports

DeLisha Milton-Jones, basketball player who has been a two-time Olympic gold medalist and two-time WNBA champion. *(1974)*

DeLisha Milton-Jones (Photo: Gerry J. Gilmore)

Tom Landry, football player and coach known for his 29-year tenure as coach of the Dallas Cowboys. *(1917)*

Carl Zeiss

Nikita Khrushchev making a toast

Who Died on September 11?

Art

Max Fleischer, pioneering animator known for the Betty Boop, Popeye, and Superman cartoon franchises.. *(1972)*

Business

Collett E. Woolman, co-founder of Delta Air Lines. *(1966)*

Ralph C. Smedley, founder of Toastmasters International. *(1948)*

Government

Salvador Allende, Marxist president of Chile, committed suicide after being overthrown in a coup led by General Augusto Pinochet, who subsequently ruled Chile as dictator. *(1973)*

Nikita Khrushchev (Никита Хрущёв), leader of the Soviet Union following the death of Joseph Stalin, removed from power in 1964 following the Cuban Missile Crisis. *(1971)*

Muhammad Ali Jinnah (محمد علی جناح), leader of the All-India Muslim League during the campaign for Indian independence; founder and first governor-general of Pakistan following independence and partition Revered in Pakistan as Great Leader *(Qayid-i-Azam)* and Father of the Nation *(Baba-i-Qaum)*. *(1948)*

Muhammad Ali Jinnah (left), with Gandhi (1944)

Music

Bob Crewe, songwriter and record producer who wrote such hits as "Big Girls Don't Cry," "Walk Like a Man," and "Can't Take My Eyes Off You." *(2014)*

Peter Tosh, Jamaican reggae musician who began as a member of Bob Marley's band The Wailers before embarking on a successful solo career. *(1987)*

Performing Arts

Kevin McCarthy, actor best known as the male lead in *Invasion of the Body Snatchers* (1956); earned a Golden Globe and an Oscar nomination for his role in *Death of a Salesman* (1951).

Harold Gould, known for roles in the film *The Sting,* and television series *Rhoda* and *The Golden Girls.* *(2010)*

Larry Gelbart, television producer and writer best known for the long-running television series *M*A*S*H.* (2009)

John Ritter, television actor known for *Three's Company* and *8 Simple Rules.* (2003)

Kim Hunter, received an Oscar and a Golden Globe for *A Streetcar Named Desire* (1951), also appeared in the soap opera *The Edge of Night* and as Zira in the first three *Planet of the Apes* films. *(2002)*

Jessica Tandy, stage and film actress, films include *Cocoon, Driving Miss Daisy* (for which she received the Best Actress Oscar), and *Fried Green Tomatoes. (1994)*

Lorne Greene, actor best known as the father on the TV series *Bonanza,* and as Commander Adama in *Battlestar Galactica* and *Galactica 1980. (1987)*

Science and Medicine

Janet Parker, British medical photographer who became the last recorded person to die from smallpox during the 1978 smallpox outbreak in the United Kingdom. *(1978)*

Sports

Johnny Unitas, record-setting football quarterback primarily with the Baltimore Colts, member of the Pro Football Hall of Fame. *(2002)*

Writing

Lois Lenski, award-winning author and illustrator of children's books, including the classic *Strawberry Girl (1974)*

Lorne Greene as Ben Cartwright in *Bonanza*

Quote of the Day

"Politicians are the same all over.
They promise to build a bridge even
where there is no river."

Nikita Khrushchev (Никита Хрущёв)
leader of the Soviet Union
died September 11, 1971

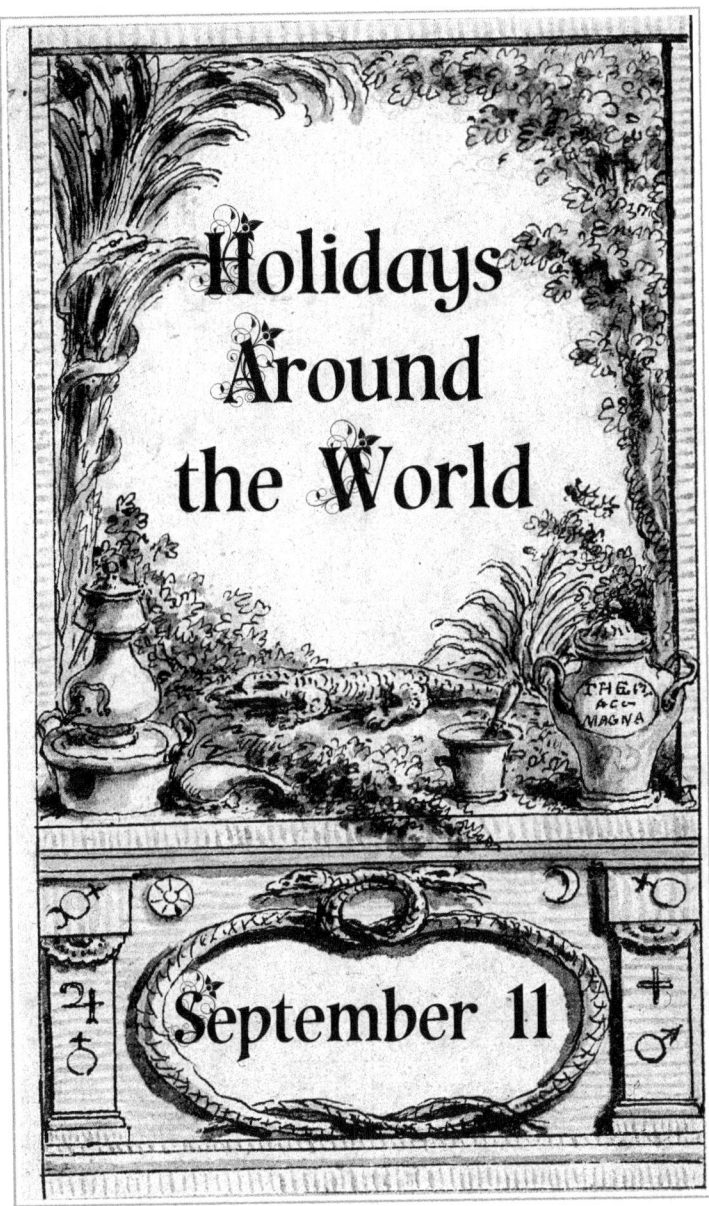

Holidays
Around
the World

September 11

Michael Dobson

A photograph of the 2012 Tribute in Light, with two beams of light
substituting for the destroyed Twin Towers — for **Patriot Day**
(Photo: "Jackie," CC BY-SA 2.0)

Holidays Around the World

If you're looking for a reason to take your special day off, you should know that every single day is a holiday somewhere in the world! Here's what you can celebrate on September 11!

General Events

9-1-1 Emergency Number Day (United States)
First proclaimed by President Ronald Reagan in 1987, this day recognizes the public safety benefits provided by emergency telephone numbers.

Battle of Tendra Day (Russia)
The Russian armed forces observe memorable victories in their history on the Days of Military Honour (Дни воинской славы, *dni voinskoy slavy*). September 11 commemorates the naval Battle of Tendra, which took place in 1790 durring the Russo-Turkish War.

Enkutatash (እንቁጣጣሽ) (Ethiopia)

September 11 (September 12 in leap years) is New Year's Day (Mäskäräm 1) according to the Ethiopian calendar, which derives from the Coptic Church calendar used in Egypt and elsewhere..

National Day of Catalonia (Catalonia, Spain)

The National Day of Catalonia commemorates the the fall of Barcelona on September 11, 1714, and the subsequent loss of Catalonian independence.

Patriot Day (United States)

The National Day of Service and Remembrance, or Patriot Day, honors the memory of those killed in the 2001 attacks. A number of related observances also occur on this day. (Photo page 36.)

Teacher's Day (Argentina)

Many nations set aside a day to honor schoolteachers. In Argentina, Teacher's Day in Argentina honors President Domingo Faustino Sarmiento (died September 11, 1888), who established a comprehensive educational system in that nation.

Food Holidays

Around the world, days, weeks, and months are dedicated to certain foods. In the United States, there's an official food day for every day of the year!. Given the wide range of foods, often multiple foods share the same occasion. Food days are sponsored by manufacturers, retailers, farmers, fans, and occasionally by proclamation, and are subject to change.

September 11 is **National Hot Cross Bun Day.** Hot cross buns are spiced sweet buns with raisins or currants, and are traditionally eaten on Good Friday, which isn't anywhere near September 11. In fact, during the reign of Queen Elizabeth I of England, it was illegal to sell hot cross buns except at burials, on Good Friday, or for Christmas!

Hot Cross Buns (Photo: Punzy)

Food Months

The entire month of September is used to celebrate numerous foods. Here's a list of what to eat in the month of September!

- Bourbon Heritage Month
- California Wine Month
- National Chicken Month
- National Honey Month
- National Mushroom Month
- National Papaya Month
- National Potato Month
- National Rice Month
- National Whole Grains Month
- National Wild Rice Month

A glass and bottle of bourbon, for Bourbon Heritage Month
(Photo: Dirk Ingo Franke)

Religious Observances

Auditor's Day (Scientology)
The Church of Scientology honors its auditors on the second Sunday in September, which occurs on September 11 in some years.

Nayrouz (Coptic Orthodox Church)
Celebrated on the first day of the Coptic New Year (September 11, September 12 in leap years), Nayrouz commemorates martyrs and confessors of the church.

A Coptic Orthodox icon of Christ (Courtesy: Louvre Museum)

Saint Days (Christianity)

Each day in the year is considered a feast day for one or more saints. They are somewhat different in western Christianity (Catholicism and many forms of Protestantism) and in eastern (Orthodox) Christianity. There are many others; this is a selection.

In *Western Christianity*, it is the feast day of Saints Deiniol, Harry Burleigh (Episcopal Church), John Gabriel Perboyre, Our Lade of Coromoto, Paphnutius of Thebes, Protus, and Hyacinth.

In *Eastern Orthodox Christianity*, it is also the commemoration of Saints Euphrosynus the Cook of Alexandria, Felix and Regula, Patiens of Lyon, Emilian, Vincent of Léon, Almirus, Adelphus, Bodo, and John the Abbot of Svyatogorsk Monastery. (These are observed on August 29 by "Old Calendarists †.")

Honorary Months

Presidents, Congresses, and nations around the world issue proclamations recognizing particular months to honor certain causes. These events generally fall in Septemer, though honorary months do come and go. Holidays established by states and nonprofit organizations are listed if verified. If not otherwise specified, all are US. TTwo places to get up to date information are the current edition of Chase's Calendar of Events *or the website* Brownielocks.

---

† "Old Calendrists" use the Julian calendar rather than the modern Gregorian calendar. See "What Day of the Week is September 11?"

- Baby Safety Month
- Be Kind to Editors and Writers Month
- Children's Good Manners Month
- College Savings Month
- Happy Cat Month
- International Square Dancing Month
- National Recovery Month
- National Service Dog Month
- Responsible Dog Ownership Month

Moveable and Multi-Day Events

Some events take place over a specific week or time period. Start and finish dates may vary from year to year. Some events occur on different days each year (such as "fourth Saturday of a month"). These events sometimes take place on September 11.

First Monday After Labor Day
- National Boss/Employee Exchange Day

Second Sunday in September
- Father's Day (Latvia)
- National Grandparent's Day (Estonia, United States)
- Racial Justice Day (British churches)
- Tanker's Day (Russia)
- Turkmen Bakhshi Day (Turkmenistan)

Nearest Weekday to September 12
- Saragarhi Day (Sikhs)

Week Including September 17
- Celebrate Freedom Week (Kansas, Texas)

Quote of the Day

"Never trust the artist. Trust the tale."

D. H. Lawrence, novelist
born September 11, 1885

About the Month of

September

September, from the *Brevarium Grimani* by Simon Bening (c.1510)

September: The Ninth Month

The morrow was a bright September morn;
The earth was beautiful as if new-born;
There was that nameless splendor everywhere,
That wild exhilaration in the air,
Which makes the passers in the city street
Congratulate each other as they meet.

Henry Wadsworth Longfellow, "Tales of a Wayside Inn"

In Latin, *septem* means "seven," so it may seem strange that September is actually the *ninth* month of the year. The original Roman calendar, on which ours is based, started in March, making September indeed the seventh month. No one is completely sure when the start of the year was moved to January, but the traditional name of September stuck.

Romans also associated September with the god Vulcan, and thus expected the month to have fires, volcanic eruptions, and earthquakes.

In the northern hemisphere, September marks the beginning of meteorological autumn. In the southern hemisphere, September is the seasonal equivalent of March, the beginning of spring.

September and December always begin on the same day of the week. However, no other month in the same year will end on the same day of the week as September.

For countries that switched from the Julian to the Gregorian calendars in 1752, the date jumped from September 2 to September 14, meaning that there is no September 11 in that year.

September in Other Cultures

In Old English, the month of September was known as
Hāligmōnaþ. Anglo-Saxons called it *Gerst monath*
(Barley month) celebrating the barley harvest that
would shortly be turned into beer. In Finland, it is
syyskuu, in Poland *wrzesień*, and in Greece
Σεπτέμβριος. The Russians call the month сентябрь.
While both the Hebrew and Arabic cultures have their
own calendar system, the Hebrew word for
"September" is ספטמבר and in Arabic it's سبتمب. The
Azerbaijani call the month *Sentyabr*. In Hindi, the
month of "sitambar" is written सितंबर. In both China
and Japan, it's known as 九月, 구월 in Korea, and 腩尬
in Vietnam.

September Sayings and Superstitions

Here are some wedding sayings and superstitions
associated with the month of September.

- "Marry in September's shrine, your living with
  be rich and fine."
- "A September bride will be discreet, affable, and
  much liked."
- "Married in September's golden glow/Smooth
  and serene your life will go."

As for which day of the week, that's easy.

Monday for health, Tuesday for wealth,
Wednesday best of all, Thursday for losses,
Friday for crosses, Saturday for no luck at all.

September Symbols

Birthstone: Sapphire, representing clear thinking.

Star sapphire

Birth Flowers: Forget-me-not, morning glory, and aster.

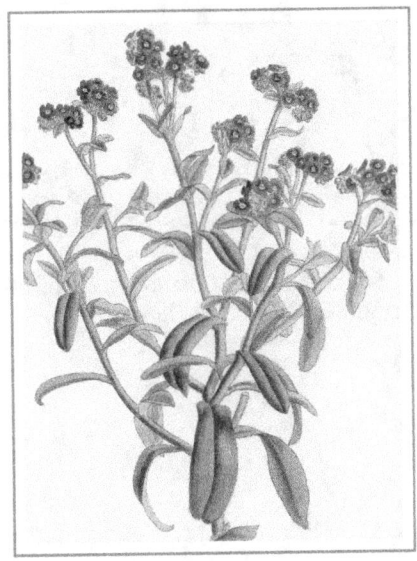

Forget-me-not (*moyosotis azorica*)

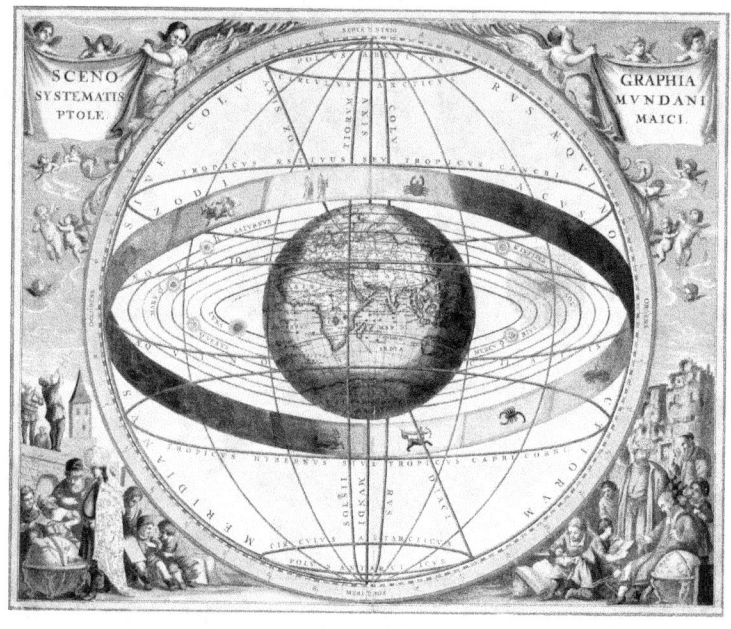

Scenography of the Ptolemaic Cosmography, by Johannes van Loon, based on Andreas Cellarius's *Harmonia Macrocosmica,* 1660

September 11 Zodiac Signs

From the perspective of someone on Earth, the Sun appears to move through the sky throughout the year, along a path astronomers call the *ecliptic plane*. The ecliptic plane is divided into twelve constellations, known as the zodiac, based on traditionally observed patterns of stars. On your birthday, you can't see your constellation, because it's in the daytime sky.

The zodiac was first developed by Babylonian astronomers about 2,500 years ago. Because they were unaware that the Earth wobbles like a spinning top (known as *precession*), they didn't make allowance for the fact that the Sun's path through the zodiac changes over time.

That means there are now two sets of dates for your birth sign. The *tropical dates* are the original Babylonian dates; the *sidereal dates* tell you where the Sun actually appears as it moves along its annual path.

For September 11, the tropical sign is **Virgo** and the sidereal sign is **Leo**.

Leo

Tropical July 23 to August 23
Sidereal August 16 to September 15

In Greek mythology, Leo, the lion, was killed by Hercules during one of his twelve labors. The easiest part of Leo to see in the night sky is an asterism known as the Sickle, looking a bit like a backward question mark. One of the nearest stars to Earth, Wolf 359 (just under eight light-years away), can be found in Leo.

In astrology, Leo is considered to be a fire sign. Traits associated with Leo are generosity, warmth, brightness, and self-motivation. Leos are supposed to be compatible with Aries and Sagittarius, and to a lesser extent with Gemini, Libra, and Aquarius.

Virgo

Tropical August 23 to September 22
Sidereal September 16 to October 15

The constellation Virgo is the second-largest constellation in the night sky. Its brightest star, Spica, makes it easy to locate. If you can find the Big Dipper (Ursa Major), follow the curve in the Dipper's handle. The second bright star you see is Spica.

In Greek and Roman mythology, Virgo is associated with Demeter (Ceres), the goddess of wheat, and also with Erigone and Astraea. In astrology, Virgo is known as a "mutable sign." It's associated with being reflective and receptive to the ideas of others, sensitive to criticism, and oriented toward detail and precision.

Virgos are supposed to be compatible with Capricorn, Taurus, Cancer, and Scorpio, and to a lesser extent with Virgo and Pisces.

Illustration by Edward Penfield

What Day of the Week is September 11?

On what day of the week does September 11 fall?

Surprisingly, this isn't an easy question. Because the calendar year is 365 days long (366 in leap years), it doesn't divide evenly by the seven days of the week.

Also, the Earth goes around the Sun in about 365-1/4 days, so a calendar tends to drift over time. That's why the same date falls on different weekdays in different years.

This is made even more complicated by a change in calendars that took place in 1582. Our modern calendar has its roots in ancient Rome, in a calendar reform conducted by Julius Caesar. Caesar commissioned mathematicians to attack the problem, and they came up with the idea of leap years, and thus standardized the calendar for centuries to come. This was called the Julian calendar.

Over time, however, the small errors in Caesar's calculation compounded. That's why Pope Gregory XIII commissioned the Gregorian calendar, used in most of the world today. Some countries converted in 1582, when the calendar was first developed; some converted later; other still haven't changed.

Gregorian and Julian aren't the only types of calendars. The Hebrew year, the Islamic year, and many other calendars are used in different parts of the world and among different people.

You can convert Gregorian dates to other calendars, including the Hebrew calendar, the Islamic calendar, and even the Mayan calendar by visiting the Fourmilab Calendar Converter at http://www.fourmilab.ch/documents/calendar/.

Chinese calendar systems are quite complex and have changed several times; a full discussion is far beyond the scope of this book. If you're interested, you can find information here: http://www.hermetic.ch/cal_stud/chinese_cal.htm.

On Names and Dates

Historians use "CE" (Common Era) and "BCE" (Before the Common Era) instead of the more common "AD" (Anno Domini, or Year of Our Lord) and "BC" (Before Christ), reflecting the fact that the year-numbering system established by the Gregorian calendar is used throughout the world in many countries not culturally Christian.

The CE/BCE designation dates back to at least 1708, and has been adopted as a standard by the United Nations and the Universal Postal Union. Because this series of books covers events and people of all nations and cultures, we use the CE/BCE terms.

The abbreviation "O.S." ("Old Style") on some dates refers to the fact that the Russian Empire did not switch from the Julian to the Gregorian calendar at the same time as the rest of Europe, and therefore some figures and events have two dates.

Also, in the Julian calendar in England in the 16th century, the year began on March 25 rather than January 1. To avoid confusion with Gregorian dates, dates between January and March were often written using both years.

People and events whose original names are not in the Western alphabet have their native names (where possible) in the appropriate script shown in parenthesis. If you are using an e-reader to access an electronic version of this book, all characters don't always display on all devices.

A 50-year brass perpetual calendar.

Quote of the Day

"Time is an illusion, lunchtime doubly so."

Douglas Adams,
from *The Hitchhiker's Guide to the Galaxy*

Notes and Credits

Timespinner Press

THEM ACC MAGNA

Cartoon by John T. McCutcheon

Copyright, Credit, and Contact

Dedication

This volume of *The Story of a Special Day* is dedicated to my father, Odell Dobson, a waist gunner on "Ford's Folly," a B-24 Liberator in World War II. It was shot down over Koblenz, Germany, on September 11, 1944. My father was one of two survivors, and was subsequently captured by the Germans and made a prisoner of war. His story in his own words can be found as a free PDF download at http://tinyurl.com/rj5Dobson.

Follow Us

Our blog "This Day in History" (http://timespinnerpress.com/this-day-in-history/) features short articles on events and people associated with each day, and updates several times each week. Also subscribe to the "Quote of the Day" at http://timespinnerpress.com/quote-of-the-day/. You can get daily links by following us on Facebook at TimespinnerPress, or on Twitter as @sidewisethinker.

Contact Us

Find an error or a format problem? Want information about the series, about us, or about when the volume for your special day might be available? Please email us at editor@timespinnerpress.com. (We also take requests if your special day isn't yet complete. Please give us at least six weeks' notice if possible.)

Sources

We owe a great debt to Wikipedia, which is our first stop for research. We attempt to make independent confirmation of all important dates and facts through a variety of other sources.

Other sources we frequently use include the Library of Congress; "on this day" listings from *Encyclopedia Britannica*, the *New York Times*, and the BBC; Omniglot for the names of months in other languages; *Chase's Calendar of Events*; Brownielocks.com, Foodimentary, and, of course, the always essential Google.

All art and photographs are either in the public domain, used under a Creative Commons license, or with a "fair use" justification, and most frequently come from Wikimedia Commons and the Library of Congress Prints and Photographs Division.

Attribution is provided where possible, or as requested by the copyright owner, or when there is particular historical significance, listed below. For information about any particular illustration or photograph, please contact us.

Credits

1. The cover photograph of the World Trade Towers on September 11, 2001, is part of a collection received from the New York District Attorney's Office from an unattributed photographer. According to Wikimedia Commons, its author, Mike Goad, has released this work into the public domain worldwide. It has been cropped to fit the cover dimensions.

2. The illustration of the month of September used on the back cover is from the French Gothic illuminated manuscript *Les Très Riches Heures du duc de Berry* by the Limbourg Brothers, Jean Colombe, and an intermediate painter whose name is

lost to history. It is in the public domain because its copyright has expired.

3. The box graphic used on the first page is from a 1916 pamphlet entitled "Divorce versus Democracy" authored by G. K. Chesterton, originally published in London by the Society of St. Peter and St. Paul. It is in the public domain in the US because it was published prior to 1923, and is in the public domain in all countries (including the country of origin) in which the copyright time is the author's life plus 70 years or less.

4. The graphic design for the section pages in this book is from a design originally created for a pharmacy label. It is courtesy of Wellcome Images (ICV No 11073, photo V0010813), and is used here under CC BY-SA 4.0.

5. The photograph of firefighters at the World Trade Center on 9/11 is cropped from a larger photograph. That picture is part of a collection from an unattributed photographer. According to the Library of Congress (digital ID ppmsca. 02121), it is in the public domain as a work created by an officer or employee of the US federal government as part of that person's official duties.

6. The map showing the flight paths of hijacked planes on 9/11 is courtesy of the Federal Bureau of Investigation, and is in the public domain as a work created by an officer or employee of the US federal government as part of that person's official duties.

7. The photograph of firefighters at the Pentagon 9/11 crash was taken by Marine Corporal Jason Ingersoll. It is in the public domain as a work created by an officer or employee of the US federal government as part of that person's official duties.

8. The 2011 photograph of One World Trade Center was taken by Kai Brinker, and is used here under CC BY-SA 2.0.

9. The 2008 sketch of the Golden Fleece (of the Color Adornment) showing the "French Blue" diamond and the "Côte de Bretagne" dragon spinel of king Louis XV of France is by François Farges, and is used here under CC BY-SA 3.0.

10. The 1971 photograph of General Augusto Pinochet is from the Biblioteca del Congreso Nacional de Chile, and is used here under CC BY-SA 3.0 Chile.

11. The 1971 photograph of Salvador Allende is from the Biblioteca del Congreso Nacional de Chile, and is used here under CC BY-SA 3.0 Chile. It has been cropped.

12. The Moldovan postage stamp honoring Gherman Titov is not protected by copyright according to the Republic of Moldova Law on Copyright no. 139, July 2, 2010.

13. The detail from the 1507 map by Martin Waldseemüller featuring the word "America" in print for the first time is courtesy Library of Congress. It is in the public domain because its copyright has expired.

14. The photograph of William Sydney Porter (O. Henry) first appeared in the book *Analyzing Character,* by A. Newcomb and K. M. H. Blackford in 1922. It is in the public domain because its copyright has expired.

15. The 2014 photograph of Harry Connick, Jr., is by "bg_nh2014," and is used here under CC BY-SA 3.0.

16. The 1973 photograph of Lola Falana and Gino Bramieri in the Italian television show *Hai visto mai?* first appeared in the magazine *Radiocorriere.* It is in the public domain in Italy because its copyright has expired, according to the Law for the Protection of Copyright and Neighbouring Rights n.633, 22 April 1941.

17. The publicity photograph of Kristy McNichol from the television series *Family* is in the public domain because it was first published in the United States between 1923 and 1977 without a copyright notice. Typically, publicity photographs are not copyrighted because of the way in which they are intended to be used.

18. The 1979 photograph of Ferdinand and Imelda Marcos was taken by Al Ramones and Domie Quiazon of the US Army. It is in the public domain as a work created by an officer or employee of the US federal government as part of that person's official duties.

19. The 2007 photograph of DeLisha Milton-Jones was taken by Gerry J. Gilmore. It is in the public domain as a work created by an officer or employee of the US federal government as part of that person's official duties.

20. The photograph of Carl Zeiss was released by the Carl Zeiss Company, and is used here under CC BY-SA 2.0.

21. The 1944 photograph of Muhammad Ali Jinnah and Mohandas K. Gandhi is courtesy of the British Library (photo 429/17). It is in the public domain because its copyright has expired according to the Indian Copyright Act of 1957.

22. The publicity photograph of Lorne Greene from the television series *Bonanza* is in the public domain because it was first published in the United States between 1923 and 1977 without a copyright notice. Typically, publicity photographs are not copyrighted because of the way in which they are intended to be used.

23. The 2005 photograph of the Twin Lights in New York City was taken by "Jackie," and is used here under CC BY-SA 2.0.

24. The 911 Emergency Sign is in the public domain, as are all traffic signs.

25. The 2007 photograph of hot cross buns is by "Punzy," and is used here under CC BY-SA 2.0.

26. The 8th century Coptic icon of Christ is from the collection of the Louvre Museum (AF 11565). It is in the public domain because its copyright has expired.

27. The painting "September" is from the *Brevarium Grimani,* circa 1510, and is in the public domain because its copyright has expired.

28. The photograph of a star sapphire was released into the public domain by its author, Mitchell Gore.

29. The chromolithograph of a forget-me-not is by Louis-Aristide Léon Constans and originally appeared in the 1852-1853 edition of *Paxton's Flower Garden.* It is in the public domain because its copyright has expired.

30. The celestial sphere is from *Scenography of the Ptolemaic Cosmography,* by Johannes van Loon, based on Andreas Cellarius's *Harmonia Macrocosmica,* 1660. It is in the public domain because its copyright has expired.

31. The 1906 automobile calendar is by Edward Penfield, and is in the collection of the Library of Congress Prints and Photographs Division. It is in the public domain because its copyright has expired.

32. The 50-year perpetual calendar photograph is in the public domain.

33. The cartoon by John T. McCutcheon is from his 1905 collection *The Mysterious Stranger and Other Cartoons* by John T. McCutcheon. It is in the public domain because its copyright has expired.

License Description and Terms

Aside from material purely in the public domain, photographs and other material in this book are used under specific licenses permitting free use, usually with an attribution requirement. For full text and terms of these licenses, click or enter the appropriate links below. If you believe there is an error in the copyright status or attribution of any of these images, please email us.

- Creative Commons Attribution 2.0 Generic (CC-BY 2.0): http://creativecommons.org/licenses/by/2.0/deed.en
- Creative Commons Attribution-Share Alike 3.0 Generic (CC-BY-SA 3.0): http://creativecommons.org/licenses/by-sa/3.0/
- Creative Commons Attribution-Share Alike 2.5 Generic (CC-BY-SA 2.5): http://creativecommons.org/licenses/by-sa/2.5/deed.en
- Creative Commons Attribution-Share Alike 2.0 Generic (CC-BY-SA 2.0): http://creativecommons.org/licenses/by/2.0/deed.en
- Creative Commons Attribution-Share Alike 1.0 Generic (CC-BY-SA 1.0): http://creativecommons.org/licenses/by-sa/1.0/deed.en
- CC0 1.0 Universal (CC0 1.0) Public Domain Dedication (CC0 1.0) http://creativecommons.org/publicdomain/zero/1.0/deed.en
- GNU Free Documentation License (GFDL): http://en.wikipedia.org/wiki/Wikipedia:Text_of_the_GNU_Free_Documentation_License
- License Art Libre (Free Art License): http://artlibre.org

Other Books from Timespinner Press

The Story of a Special Day
Michael Dobson

A series of (eventually) 366 volumes covering everything that happened on your special day! Events, births, deaths, quotes, holidays, and much more. It's like a birthday card they'll never throw away!

US$7.95 print / US$2.99 ebook.

From Plassey to Pakistan
Humayun Mirza

The history of British Colonial India and the formation of Pakistan from the unique perspective of the son of Pakistan's first president and last of the royal line of Bengal, Bihar, and Orissa! This unique historical document tells the inside story of this distinguished family, including the detailed story of the coup that toppled his father from power!

US$27.95 print

A Whole New Navy: America's War in the Pacific

Miles Durr

The most comprehensive and detailed description of America's naval war in the Pacific ever—every battle, every ship, every task force and every task group from Pearl Harbor through the Japanese surrender! A must-have for the collection of every World War II buff!

US$29.95 print

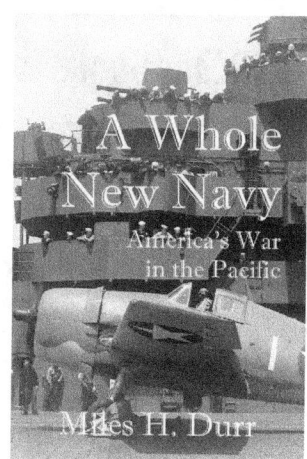

Improbable History: The Weird, the Obscure, and the Strangely Important

edited by Michael Dobson

From the birth of Western civilization to the rescue of Apollo 13, from the Leaning Tower of Pisa to Florence's Duomo, history has often turned on small, improbable details. Whatever happened to the ancient Samaritan people? Why did a fortuitous rainstorm allow the British to conquer India? How did an air raid in Italy lead to the development of chemotherapy? What happened when Albert Einstein met Adolf Hitler on the streets of Berlin? How did the Japanese manage to attack the US mainland using balloons? A cast of award-winning writers tackle some of the strangest tales in history!

US$19.95 print

www.ingramcontent.com/pod-product-compliance
Lightning Source LLC
Chambersburg PA
CBHW062107280526
45788CB00003B/1382